Soul Pursuit:
The Busy Person's Guide to
Biblical Meditation

Lynelle Watford

TABLE OF CONTENTS

APPENDICES

INTRODUCTION

"But his delight is in the law of the LORD,
and on his law he meditates day and night.
He is like a tree planted by streams of water that yields
its fruit in its season, and its leaf does not wither.
In all that he does, he prospers."
Psalms 1:2-3

You have a slim probability of meditating if the 2015 National Center for Health Statistics report is accurate. It claims that only eight percent of U.S. adults practice a form of meditation. While a variety of types of meditation exist, meditation, at its core, involves repetition of thought or speech along with reflection. Based on that concept, though, we all meditate.

Surprised? We all meditate on *something*. Self-talk dominates the conversation of our lives. Where does your inner conversation turn when you are alone, when your mind disengages, when you can't sleep at night? Probably your thoughts most naturally turn to challenges— relational demands, financial woes, or issues at work. But you *could* focus on God's Word, eternal truths, precious promises, or God's unchanging character.

Which choice will give you greater joy, peace, wisdom, strength, and comfort? In which direction would God point you? This book will help guide your thoughts to life, health, and peace.

If you yearn for something more in your life, if life has left you battered and pain-ridden, if you hunger after God, read on. Even—and especially—if you believe you can't squeeze another spiritual habit into your busy schedule, read on. Finally, if you thirst for life change, read on.

You already meditate. Let's turn your worries into delight.

1

Pursue with Perspective

"My soul will be satisfied as with fat and rich food,
and my mouth will praise you with joyful lips, when I remember you
upon my bed, and meditate on you in the watches of the night;
for you have been my help, and in the shadow of your wings
I will sing for joy."
Psalm 63:5-7

"I LOVE YOU," Trent assured me as he cradled my hand in his long fingers.

"I love you, too," I replied in a shaky voice.

Maneuvering around IV lines and an assortment of tubes, he gave me a quick, but fervent hug. Then he disappeared from my line of view.

It was about 11 p.m. on February 24, 1990. Trent and I found ourselves alone, in an unfamiliar city. One hundred fifty miles away, my parents cared for our two boys—two-week-old Nathan and three-year-old Jonathan. A sense of isolation threatened to overwhelm me as orderlies wheeled me down sterile halls, through double doors, and finally into surgery.

I knew I may never see Trent again.

Earlier that day, the doctors ruled out surgery, and then later determined they must operate despite a forty percent chance I would not survive.

"We need to remove that hematoma or she won't make it," the head doctor informed us.

This can't be happening! I just came in to have a baby. As frantic as a caged animal, an urge to rip out IV lines and escape from intensive care nearly pushed me to action. *I have to get home. My boys need me.*

But I knew that, in my weakened condition, I didn't have strength to take two steps. Besides, all that day spasms, induced by the pressure of the nearly two-liter sized, growing blood clot convinced me I desperately needed medical treatment. Our local hospital, unable to give me the care I needed, had me airlifted to University of Michigan Hospital.

The voice of reason soon quieted my heart.

During the hour wait before surgery, Trent and I had exchanged last words, and I dictated messages for my parents and children in the event I didn't live.

Now in the operating room, a sense of aloneness *should* have engulfed me—except for one thing. In past years, I had committed large portions of scripture to memory. As my source for meditation, I clung to them, especially at night. Now treasured friends, these rock-solid truths assured me that God Himself drew near. Verses such as these two favorites:

Psalm 27:1 – *"The LORD is my light and my salvation; whom shall I fear? The LORD is the stronghold of my life; of whom shall I be afraid?"*

Isaiah 40:29 – *"He gives power to the faint, and to him who has no might he increases strength."*

Those words permeated my mind and enveloped my heart in peace as I awaited my surgery. Calmly, I faced the uncertain future.

Why Meditate?

Have you considered meditating on scripture? Are you aware of the invaluable benefits meditation can bring to your life? No doubt you have heard Bible verses such as these Old Testament standards:

Joshua 1:8 – *"This Book of the Law shall not depart from your mouth, but you shall meditate on it day and night, so that you may be careful to do according to all that is written in it. For then you will make your way prosperous, and then you will have good success."*

Psalm 1:2 – *"But his delight is in the law of the LORD, and on his law he meditates day and night."*

The New Testament also speaks of filling our minds with God's Word:

Colossians 3:16 instructs us, *"Let the word of Christ dwell in you richly, teaching and admonishing one another in all wisdom, singing psalms and hymns and spiritual songs, with thankfulness in your hearts to God."*

John 15:7 advises, *"If you abide in me, and my words abide in you, ask whatever you wish, and it will done for you."*

A few months ago, I talked to my friend Joyce several times about meditation and this book as I worked on it. Joyce's family was grappling with a difficult situation, and she faced an upcoming court appearance. The day after the Friday hearing, Joyce related what had happened.

A phone call on Thursday evening from the attorney revealed the exact purpose of the hearing. The ramifications of the hearing on those she loved and the potential effect of her testimony weighed heavily on Joyce. Her trepidation led her to commit her concerns to God, and she fervently prayed for wisdom.

The next day tested Joyce's ability to wait. Once at the courthouse, she remained with others in the hall for over an hour and a half. Then a bailiff called the others in, but she was left alone until her turn to testify.

Anxious and desperate for a favorable outcome, she looked to divert her mind from imaginations of what may be transpiring in the courtroom. No purse, no phone, no magazines. What could she do?

This place of silence could be a perfect opportunity to meditate, she realized. One at a time, Joyce reflected on verses she could recall from memory. She contemplated the significance of each word and how it applied to her situation. Then she prayed with those thoughts in mind.

She repeated this process for the next seventy-five minutes until the court broke for lunch. Within the sterile environment of the courthouse hall and her inner anguish, scripture had brought a slice of heaven into the depths of her being. God's Word blanketed her heart and mind, creating an unexpected calmness and a confidence that God would help her remember what she wanted to say.

After lunch and another wait, a bailiff finally called Joyce into the courtroom. He led her to the witness stand in full view of loved ones, witnesses, attorneys, and the judge. She could have felt intimidated and paralyzed at the import of her testimony, but instead calmness reigned. She spoke the truth with boldness and tempered with love, though uncomplimentary at times. The defense cross-examined her and tried two times to make her look or feel unreasonable. She countered with clarity of thought and full composure.

Finally, the hearing ended and with it came relief—relief the hearing was over and how well her testimony had gone. Meditation on God's Word had made a key difference in the state of her heart and mind, which in turn had a positive impact on her responses and words. Her spirit overflowed with thanksgiving.

A Story of Beginnings

Let me tell you why I choose to meditate.

God uses meditation, a spiritually dynamic practice, in my life as He makes me more like Jesus. It still amazes me how reflecting on the Bible transforms me—my thoughts, emotions, words, and motivations.

Twenty-three years after my risky surgery, fears often plagued me. I feared that tragedy would fall on my husband or our older son, Jonathan, an Air Force pilot.

Jonathan lived in England, but we usually communicated with him once a week via FaceTime. In between times, we could email. Sometimes, if he was on a mission, we didn't FaceTime and responses to our emails could be delayed.

Something must have happened. Why else didn't he email? How could I take it if something happens to him? These thoughts and more would hijack my mind, flooding my heart with fear and tightening my stomach into knots.

I responded the same when Trent would be late coming home from a job or from bike riding. Especially if calls to his cell phone resulted in, "This is Trent Watford of Tech Help. Please leave a message." Dread and anxiety held me captive.

My fears were not totally unfounded.

Three years earlier, in 2010, we lived through one of the worst nightmares a parent can experience. At age twenty, our younger son, Nathan, tragically died while stationed in Guam with the Navy. He died by suicide. After that experience, I knew that horrific tragedies didn't just happen to other people. They could—and would—happen to me as well.

Fear blighted my journal entries. I knew I needed to trust God more. I read the Bible. I prayed. I memorized. I even meditated ... some. But apprehension still had the upper hand. Slowly I began to sense a need for significant change in my life.

My habits of memorization and meditation had become sketchy at best. When Nathan died, grief impaired my memory and I never totally regained it. At night I would turn to meditation, but could only recollect a few verses.

My journal entry from January 8, 2015, summarizes it well: *Is it any wonder that fear haunts me? I know deep down I am not immune from the most painful losses that life can throw at a person. What if it happens again? And again? And again?*

Just the day before, I had listened to a podcast by mistake. If I had known the topic was memorization, I would have made another selection. I knew all about memorization (so I thought). I just didn't discipline my mind to actually do it. *Life is hard enough as it is. My mind just needs a break.*

Through the *Revive Our Hearts* broadcast (January 7, 2015), I realized that my problem wasn't lack of discipline, but lack of hunger. On that broadcast, Nancy DeMoss Wolgemuth interviewed Janet Pope about Janet's book, *His Word in My Heart,* on the topic of memorizing scripture.

Janet: What if I said to you, "You're so disciplined in

eating breakfast, lunch, and dinner every single day. You rarely miss a day."

Nancy: Most of us could say that.

Janet: But you would say, "No, it's not discipline. I'm hungry." And so I would say to you, "It's not that you are lacking discipline [to memorize]. It's that you are not hungry."[i]

As I listened to this interchange about discipline, I thought, *But I am hungry. I'm desperate for God. I cannot face life without Him.* That day I got back to memorizing.

I chose to start with Psalm 1, a familiar chapter yet I could not quote it. One night, snuggled in a warm bed while snow and ice ruled the outdoor landscape, my thoughts centered on verse three: *"And he shall be like a tree planted by the rivers of water, that bringeth forth his fruit in his season; his leaf also shall not wither; and whatsoever he doeth shall prosper."* (KJV)

This comparison fascinated me: *"And he shall be like a tree planted."* I visualized God using His own hands to lovingly plant me in a place He carefully selected and which offered the best resources for wellness, growth, and fruitfulness. I pondered the implications of such actions, of His unfathomable love expressed in deliberate forethought and careful planning.

God's sovereignty (something I already knew but now examined in a fresh perspective) brought comfort and peace. Unexpectedly, a tidal wave of assurance enveloped my soul, washing away "What if's" and "I cant's." I felt confident that if something "bad" did happen to a loved one or me, God would have kindly and thoughtfully chosen that place for me. His Presence and His Word—the River of Life—would flourish right there beside me, providing all I need.

After many months of rampant fears, this insight, gleaned from immersing my heart and mind in Psalm 1:3, refreshed my soul like a spring of cool water in desert heat. And it continues to steady my emotions in the winds of change.

Biblical meditation pleases God. It also supplies our soul with rich

nourishment—with felt emotional, mental, and spi
benefits such as contentment, peace, and joy. Want to
Appendix 3 for a list of blessings from reflecting on scrip

Soul Cravings

Psalm 63:5-7 describes a satisfied soul—that is, a soul totally filled up, even to excess: "My soul will be satisfied as with fat and rich food, and my mouth will praise you with joyful lips, when I remember you upon my bed, and meditate on you in the watches of the night; for you have been my help, and in the shadow of your wings I will sing for joy."

Did you notice that the satisfied soul results "when I remember you … and meditate on you …"? But what is a soul satisfied as with fat and rich food? The phrase refers to the Lord meeting our deepest needs and longings (which only He can) just as a rich dessert satiates our physical appetite.

In his article, "The God Who Delights to Satisfy," Jonathan Berry of London, England, expresses his thoughts this way in his blog: "I confess that I have a weakness for fat and rich foods. Whether it's a full English breakfast or a chocolate indulgence cake, I find such things hard to resist. But by far my favourite of all rich foods is the delicious range of Gü puds (and no, Gü are not sponsoring this Thought for the Week). They're not cheap and are, therefore, only an occasional treat. But oh my, they are certainly very satisfying."[ii]

After reading Berry's thoughts, I couldn't resist going to gupud.com. Even their website is absolutely tantalizing. I have never been treated to a Gü pud, but I agree that a slice of decadent cheesecake is more satisfying to my taste buds than, say, apple slices.

So, what does this mean for our souls—for our inner being? We go through life foraging for scraps of love, affirmation, and attention from people. But it's never tasty or plentiful enough to quiet our gnawing appetite. When we approach God's table, it's different. God offers a banquet of love and acceptance laid out on an endless, crammed-full spread, and He encourages us to eat to the full!

We may think we crave chocolate, new clothes, a day off, or a word appreciation. But we really crave communion with God; a communion with God fostered with purposeful directing of our thoughts to scripture throughout the day and night.

Commenting on Psalm 1:2, *The Treasury of David* by Charles H. Spurgeon puts it this way: "He [the Christian] takes a text and carries it with him all day long; and in the night-watches, when sleep forsakes his eyelids, he museth upon the Word of God. In the day of his prosperity he sings psalms out of the Word of God, and in the night of his affliction he comforts himself with promises out of the same book. 'The law of the Lord' is the daily bread of the true believer."[iii]

In other words, scripture is our intimate companion, meeting our needs as they arise. God's truth realigns our pursuits, our desires, our thoughts to the eternal and away from the temporal.

In my desperate battle for life that continued even after my risky surgery, one of Trent's journal entries clearly pinpoints the importance of maintaining a memory bank of scriptures.

On March 1, 1990, he wrote, "Realized today [the] importance [of] memorizing scripture so you can use it when you are sick and can't look at your Bible."

Yes, I left the surgery room alive on February 24 after the four-hour procedure, but afterwards the doctor's voice held reserve.

"Will she survive?" Trent wanted to know.

"There's a good chance ... if we can get the bleeding to stop."

The surgery removed a large hematoma, grown in my abdomen in the previous two weeks that followed a C-section. Sometime during my pregnancy, my body developed a blood clotting disorder, violently revealed after an uneventful Cesarean section. Now the mass of blood had been removed, but nothing had corrected the underlying problem. And that was the challenge in the next few days.

I received hourly boluses (intravenous injection of a single dose of a drug over a short period) of Factor 8, one of the necessary thirteen blood clotting proteins. The resumption of dreaded plasmapheresis treatments addressed declining Factor 8 levels in my blood. (Plasmapheresis is a process for removing blood plasma without depleting the donor or patient of other blood constituents like red blood cells.)

The quagmire after the surgery appeared as hopeless as before undergoing the operation. But God's Word brought us comfort. Trent would read to me since I was too weak to read on my own, or I would recall portions from memory. Two weary, perplexed souls caught in the reality of the frailty of life, we grasped the Word of God and the God of the Word. We both realized again the importance of maintaining a treasure chest of encouraging verses in our heart and mind.

We've talked a bit about benefits of meditation. Now let's stop a moment to examine what scriptural meditation is . . . and what it isn't.

2

Invite God into Your World

"It [meditation] is a call to be thoughtful and attentive
to the God who loves you."[iv]
Kyle Strobel

FOR ONE WEEK of our honeymoon, my husband Trent and I stayed in a cabin in Paradise. Really, Paradise. In Michigan's Upper Peninsula, this tourist burg nestles up to Lake Superior, the largest of the Great Lakes. It didn't take us long to realize that Paradise attracts agate hunters. What exactly is an agate? That's just what we asked a beachcomber we met. First, though, we inquired about her search.

"I'm looking for agates. Sometimes you can find them right here on the shore," she advised with a smile and a wave at the beach.

"What is an agate?" she repeated. "Here's one I found. Do you see the rich colors and banding patterns?" She showed us an orangish stone with wavy stripes running through it. "It's actually a semi-precious gemstone. They form when liquid quartz fills an empty pocket inside another rock, usually lava."

As we parted, she challenged us with, "There are not many of them. You'll be lucky to find one."

Trent and I looked at each other and grinned. We decided to give it a try anyway. Looking for agates just gave our excursion an added dimension, more excitement. Rocks littered the beach. Could we find an agate in the expanse? We continued our lakeside stroll, enjoying each other's company, the beauty of the watery wilderness, and the fresh, crisp air.

"This might be one," Trent exclaimed as he bent down to pick up a prospect. Disappointed, he threw it into the lake.

"What about this?" I posed. I flipped the stone over to find it wasn't a keeper either. We continued our quest.

"Here's something!" Gently, I scooped the smooth stone up out of its sandy bed and studied it. Moistened from waves, its identity was obvious. We had found our agate.

Meditation, too, takes mindfulness and intentionality. Thinking God's truth invites God into our everyday moments. But meditation does not equal boring. It's a bit like living in a continual treasure hunt as we navigate through life.

A Closer Look at Meditation

Meditation. The word conjures up diverse thoughts. Dictionary.com describes it as an extended period of thought, reflection, and contemplation.[v] Sometimes it may refer to transcendental meditation or deep spiritual introspection.

What It Is and Is Not

By mediation I do not mean the eastern tradition that many pursue. Their goal focuses on peace and tranquility produced by emptying the mind. Nor do I mean seemingly meaningless repetitions of a word or phrase.

Biblical (or scriptural) meditation is simply contemplation, reflection, musing on God's Word, the Bible. Yes, scriptural meditation may result in peace and tranquility when God's Word fills our mind. It most definitely uses repetition, but in a meaningful way.

Meditation focuses on God's Word, but exactly what occurs during reflection and contemplation? Think of it this way. Take the Bible, verse by verse, phrase by phrase, word by word. Carefully exam every crevice and detail, just as a recently engaged woman gazes on her multi-faceted, sparkling diamond ring. Choose to think about Truth, God's Eternal Word, rather than our own untrue or unhealthy thoughts or thoughts generated by other mortals.

In his book about the spiritual practices of Jonathan Edwards, Kyle Strobel gives us a glimpse into what our forefathers thought about meditation. "... [M]editation is wrestling with the truth ... It is coming to grips with our sinful and rebellious heart."[vi]

Meditation is the intentional choice of life and truth over lies.

The Focus of Meditation

What does the Bible say about the habit of meditation? The Hebrew words in the Old Testament translated as a form of *meditate* (King James Version) are either: **śîyach**—to ponder, or **hâgâh**—to utter a low sound. Both words imply an ongoing process, repetition if you will. Both words refer to talk.

Whether you employ verbal speech or silent self-talk, scriptural meditation involves talk. But talk about what? In the forty-five times that these two Hebrew words appear in the Old Testament, eleven times the translator gives us the word *meditate*. Over eighty percent of the time it refers to meditation on scripture; the remaining times, on God's works. Therefore, meditation usually consists of simply speaking scripture to ourselves—aloud or silently.

Texts that refer to meditating on God and His works join many other references that don't explicitly mention a form of the word *meditation*, but refer to a similar process such as *"I remember your name in the night ..."* (Psalm 119:55) and *"I ponder the work of your hands"* (Psalm 143:5).

Reflecting on a focal point other than God's Word has some value, but has limitations.

For instance, when observing nature (God's general revelation) you could contemplate God's attributes. But general revelation offers few details about God. In contrast, scripture gives our mind a definite track to follow as opposed to unguided thoughts about God. Think driving on a road with well-defined lanes as compared to wandering on a wide runway of unmarked pavement.

You may read, hear, recite, or sing what others say about God, such as lyrics to a worship song. But others' words must always be evaluated in light of scripture. While all of these options have a place, their influence is diluted by limitations.

But most of us keep a fast-paced life and our schedules restrict the amount of time we can devote to this pursuit. For best results, you could meditate on scripture, on truth you have memorized, to carry it with you at all times, in all places you go.

Think of it this way. In his book, *Spiritual Disciplines for the Christian Life*, Donald Whitney gives this analogy in which we are the hot cup of water and the Word of God is the tea bag. "Hearing God's Word is like one dip of the tea bag into the cup. Some of the tea's flavor is absorbed by the water, but not as much as would occur with a more thorough soaking of the bag. In this analogy, reading, studying, and memorizing God's Word are represented by additional plunges of the tea bag into the cup. The more frequently the tea enters the water, the more effect it has. Meditation, however, is like immersing the bag completely and letting it steep until all the rich tea flavor has been extracted and the hot water is thoroughly tinctured reddish brown."[vii]

Meditation, the process of immersing thoughts, emotions, and will in Truth, produces treasure—a changed life.

Before meditating, I find it useful to grab a couple of tools: study and memorization.

Study

Study sounds difficult, you may think. Not really. Usually in my morning quiet time with God, I investigate a verse. Often it's a text I intend to or have already memorized.

You don't even need a bunch of books. Just open your Bible software program or Bible study website. (See Appendix 2, points 2.1 & 2.2 for resources). Navigate to your verse. Ideally, your tool will allow you to study individual words, compare the text in several versions, read various commentaries, and make notes. While not essential, verse study gives you a more complete understanding of meaning and results in the best preparation for meditation.

Memorize

Usually I memorize before I meditate. In Chapter 3, I suggest an easy method for meditation on a short text if memorization hasn't already taken place. But I prefer to memorize longer sections and especially whole chapters. Memorizing a longer passage gives a greater sense of context and, therefore, meaning.

Given enough repetition, we *will* learn. It's just how our minds work. Once you determine to memorize, you simply need to pick a method for repetition and a text to repeat.

When I began memorizing in my mid-twenties, I typed (on a typewriter) the text I wanted to memorize. I posted the document on my bathroom mirror. As I prepared for work in the morning, I looked at the verses and repeated phrase after phrase aloud until I could recite them.

In my ACC years (After the Children Came), I didn't type, I didn't write by hand, I just photocopied. I would copy pages from my Bible. These pages found their home where I spent the most time with a (sometimes) free mind: in front of the kitchen sink where I washed dishes and prepared meals.

Does noise distract your concentration? Then find those moments of quiet, even if precious few, to think God's thoughts instead of vegging out. As a young mother with rambunctious boys, I also kept my verses in plastic sleeves hanging from the shower head. I used the few minutes standing in the shower every day to review scriptures. Even with protection, I will admit that the papers had a limited life span!

These days, I print verses off from my Bible study software. For me, memorizing while preparing food or washing dishes works well, so I keep a printout in the kitchen. (We intentionally don't have a dishwasher.) And I still memorize the old-fashioned way—through repetition. Audible drills work best for me since it reinforces the words in my mind by seeing, saying, and hearing them.

Other household tasks easily facilitate memorization such as ironing, folding clothes, and mending. Sometimes I take my daily walk with verse list in hand. As a visual learner, I want to visually see the verses I'm learning.

If you have verses on 3x5 cards, take them wherever you go. Whether it's waiting at the checkout, dusting, or many other activities that do not demand your full attention, maximize those moments. Position cards in several places where you will see them often throughout the day.

Do you have an iPod Touch, smartphone, or another mobile device? Download a free Bible app with audio. Read text or listen to it. I often challenge myself to listen to already-memorized chapters, attempting to recite verses along with (or just ahead of) the audio for review purposes. But you could also listen to a passage multiple times and learn it that way.

Whatever your situation, choose a method that works for you. Try more than one way, if necessary. Determine to find a way that works. Even one verse a week, well-learned and pondered, can make a major impact in your life.

Whatever you do, don't make the mistake of concluding that you can't meditate because you can't memorize.

Time it Right

You might be wondering, *OK, that works for you, Lyn. But how will I fit meditation into my schedule?* Let's consider when you could possibly do it. God has helped us out with that one. At creation, our time was naturally split between day and night.

During the Day

Your days are super busy. Still, you have snippets of mineable time for meditation. Just contemplate on the go. Use moments your body engages in other tasks, but leaves your mind free to fill with truth. This is your prime time.

Over the years my prime time has changed. Now I use much of the time spent in the kitchen to memorize or meditate. On days I walk alone, I either review, reflect, or memorize with verse list in hand. At day's end while getting ready for bed, I review scripture.

During the Night

Darkness. Quiet. You think, *I should be sleeping*. Sometimes I have used those minutes (or hours) to pray for people. But that makes me think of their problems, sometimes creating anxiety. Not conducive to sleep. Allow my mind to wander? Not wise. My thoughts tend to think of my out-of-control to-do list. The better choice? Meditation.

Not simply a healthy sleeping potion, nighttime meditation invites the mind back toward God, to the eternal. It allows scripture to replace worry thoughts. Slow, deliberate, one-word-at-a-time review of a verse calms the mind, emotions, and spirit.

Negative emotions tend to grow out of control at night. Fears, anxieties, conflicts, needs—all seem larger than life. Physical darkness may heighten our sense of aloneness. Meditating on scripture can comfort and assure us of God's presence and love. Saturating our mind in the Word, especially at night, cuddles our needy souls in a warm cocoon of promises.

Admittedly, meditating at night has a downside. Occasionally, I will deliberately decide not to focus in depth on a verse or phrase. Instead, I will opt for a cursory review of a longer passage. Here's why. When I meditate, I often have insights or beginnings of a song or poem. Then I must rouse myself out of bed and scribble down my thoughts, hoping I can read them later. If I don't write them down immediately, they will vanish more quickly than morning dew on a hot, sunny day.

Meditation is for anytime—day or night. We don't have to cram it into an already overbooked schedule. God offers it, with open hand, as a gift we can enjoy anytime.

But before you begin this exciting process, let's look at the details.

3

Extend Intentionality
into Your Thought Life

*"You do the reflecting and let God's Spirit
do the reworking in your heart."*[viii]
Doug McIntosh

MY EMOTIONS DESPERATELY NEEDED REST as I made the 45-minute drive to an appointment several years ago. During the previous month, my mom had faced a critical health situation resulting in hospitalization, our son had deployed to Afghanistan, and my husband realized he urgently needed to look for another job. And just a month before all that, my husband and I both emerged from a nearly two-month bout with clinical depression following our younger son's death. But on that bright mid-June day, it felt good just to get out and forget some of my recent stresses.

Since mid-May, I had concentrated on studying and memorizing Psalm 31. Sometimes when I meditate, I focus so much on individual verses or phrases that I don't see the big picture. But a few days before my drive, I targeted verse nineteen: *"Oh, how abundant is your goodness, which you have stored up for those who fear you and worked for those who take refuge in you, in the sight of the children of mankind!"*

These words amazed me. Previous verses delineated the psalmist's dire straits—enemies threatened his life. Almost at the point of hopelessness, the author then breaks out with those words, *"... how abundant is your goodness ..."*! I picture it as someone who fell into a deep pit. When the prisoner believed all was lost, trapped at the bottom, he found an almost unfathomable place of peace and God's goodness.

I kept thinking about verse nineteen for the next couple of days and continued mulling it over during my 45-minute drive. As I reflected on the words, with the context in mind, I composed a little poem:

God is Holding Me

Joy can grow in the deepest valley
praise can rise in the darkest night
peace can reign in the wildest tempest
for God is holding me tight.

Hope can bloom in the driest desert
faith can soar in the dreariest day
grace can rule when strength has withered
for God keeps all of my ways.

Since then, this poem has encouraged me and others who face dark times. It all began with a hunger for God, which led to seeking Him through an intentional, protracted focus on His Word for application to my needs.

You may not consider yourself a writer or someone who would compose poems to encourage others. But could you verbally tell others about your insights?

Often I will write a poem or song from my observations, but sometimes I just come up with a one-liner. About a year ago, I took some time to reflect on Psalm 27:13: *"I believe that I shall look upon the goodness of the LORD in the land of the living!"* Then this thought came to mind: *Walk through the disappointments ... the disasters, enter the door of brokenness, and find ... LIFE.*

Or I may think of a prayer. This occurred to me as I reflected on Who God is while watering flowers one evening: *O God of creation, Who gives us each breath we take, Who feels each pain in our hearts, Who knows our every thought and motive, impart to us Your mercy and comfort that we may be trophies of Your grace and love.* Whatever my gleanings, I record them and later often share them with others in gift books, greeting cards, social media, or email.

I could give scores of other examples of how immersing in scripture has uplifted me as well as others with whom I shared my insights.

How It Looks in My Life

When first introduced to biblical meditation many years ago, I learned several steps to the process.[ix] I took those ideas, simplified them, and tailored them to my lifestyle. Over time my method has changed a bit, but I don't focus on form. Instead, I emphasize acquiring mega doses of God's Word for life change.

I don't have a neat three-step process. In fact, I utilize four (mostly quick) phases. Like so-called stages of grief, the order of these phases may change or overlap. I'll give these steps in what I consider the ideal order. Keep the big picture of life change in view. I share my system, not as a rigid road to follow, but as an example of how easy it is to incorporate meditation into a busy lifestyle. You may want to try the method and see how it works for you. Then, change it as needed.

First I choose a verse. Usually I work through a passage verse by verse. Sometimes I choose a text by topic. Earlier this year, I picked out sections about meditation. As I write this, I am focusing on John 15.

Then I study. I read the context, preferably the entire chapter or surrounding chapters. Using free e-Sword Bible software, I scrutinize main words and record my findings in the study notes section. Then I look at other translations, making note of ones that seem to reword the text best according to the word definitions I just studied. I'll record some of my observations, copy and paste some sections from commentaries that especially speak to me, and maybe write something from my heart. Before, during, and after, I ask God to *"Open my eyes, that I may behold wondrous things out of your law"* (Psalm 119:18).

Next, I memorize. If it's a single verse I am focusing on and didn't get it memorized during study time, I will print out several copies to place around my house. Then I see it during the day and learn it one phrase at a time. Before I begin a longer passage, I will print the entire section out and post it around the house. If I already have it nailed down, I'm good to go. Even during this step, the words themselves often bring a smile to my face and a little squirt of joy to my heart.

Now comes the best part. Finally, I meditate. It can be done 24/7, in any setting, with any decibel level in one's surroundings. I use snatches of seconds or stretches of many minutes. Thoughtfully, I repeat the verse aloud or in my mind. I emphasize each word, one word at a time as I repeat it. I think of the context (which I read as part of my study). I recall what the words mean. I consider other verses that relate. I wonder about questions that I have.

During this phase I see fruit, the frosting on the cake. Sometimes it's a unique insight. Or, as in the example in Chapter 1 about Psalm 1:3, it may meet a deep, long-standing need. Often it gives peace, comfort, or wisdom. And, yes, at times it brings conviction. Whatever results, it's all valuable and a source of joy and life for the soul.

A word of caution. I do not believe God 'inspires' our thoughts as scripture is inspired. Any thoughts that result from meditation must harmonize with the meaning of the verse and with the Bible as a whole. God's Word always has authority over any insights we may have.

Now you know my simple process. Let's look at how others approach meditation.

Others Speak

My method may seem too simple for you. Others have different approaches, just as valid. Maybe one of them would meet your needs better. Or maybe you'd like to pick and choose elements from more than one source. Most importantly, set the goal of having God's Word on your mind and applied to your life as much as possible.

Steps from the Institute in Basic Life Principles include: worship, study, asking questions, personalization, attentiveness to each word, illustration of main concepts, and response to God. (See Appendix 2, point 3.1 to see a link to their article on meditation and to get their meditation worksheet.)

(In recent years, allegations of abuse have been directed at the founder of Institute in Basic Life Principles, Bill Gothard. While Gothard admits some guilt, this does not negate the truths he shared or truth shared on the IBLP website.)[x]

In the article, *Biblical Meditation*, J. Hampton Keathley, III views meditation this way: "There are three things that must go together in biblical meditation: READING, REFLECTING, and RESPONDING."[xi] He advises: Read reverently, repeatedly, creatively, with study tools in hand, with understanding. Reflect purposefully, imaginatively, humbly, prayerfully, patiently. Respond with confession, faith, and obedience. (See Appendix 2, point 3.2)

An integral component of Janet Pope's method of memorization involves review. During review, she meditates. She uses scheduled times—during her morning walk, getting ready for the day, and getting ready for bed in the evening. In addition, she maximizes time in the car, waiting times, and when she attends to housework. While reviewing words in a passage, she thinks about the meaning, asks herself questions for insight and application, chews it over and over, invites God into it, and uses it as a basis for self-examination. Janet discloses, "I fill my life with a lot of silence. In the car, I turn the radio off. I use that time to think about scripture."[xii] (See Appendix 2, point 3.3)

We could mention other approaches to meditation, but now you have enough information to choose a method and try it for yourself.

Decide for Yourself

Do you see the life-changing power and potential of meditation? Are you ready to exchange your random thoughts for God's eternal thoughts? If so, let's begin the adventure!

Evaluate Your Needs and Goals

To minimize the chance of a false start, think about what you hunger after. At a buffet, you don't choose baked cod if you crave chicken nuggets (unless the last report from your bathroom scales haunts you!). Take a moment to consider your needs, to set your goals.

Do you have a need to trust God more? Desire peace in unstable circumstances? Seek assurance that God loves you? Think about your spiritual goals. Would you like to express more gratitude, have more wisdom, or love more consistently? Choose verses that speak to these specific needs. If you need a little help finding them, use your Bible study software or see the online resources in Appendix 2, point 2.2.

List the Possibilities

Have life circumstances created a hunger to cling to God? Psalm 27 has some great sections that will minister to you. Do you sense a need to seek Christ, break free from old ways, and walk in freedom? Colossians 3 packs a lot of great theology and instruction into its twenty-five verses. Maybe you carry a heavy heart and distracted mind, so a shorter passage fits your needs better. Reach for Psalm 23, so familiar and comforting.

Make a list of feasible verses or passages you may want to memorize. Save the list even after you make your first selection. Then when you are ready for your next section, you already have an inventory of prospects. Add other possibilities as you think of, hear, or read passages that suit you.

"Most of my memorization has been out of the Psalms," I recently confided to a friend, "and I would meditate in search of comfort. But recently I've meditated on a variety of scriptures."

"You shouldn't feel badly about having concentrated on the Psalms. In that season of your life you needed comfort," my friend reassured me.

She was right. Even from way back, the Psalms attracted me. I resonated with the psalmist's desperation for God because I, too, lived with difficult situations—chronic pain from rheumatoid arthritis, for one.

Even this year, I have again gone back to the Psalms. These 150 chapters formed the Psalter for God's people from Old Testament times to Martin Luther's day and beyond. More than any other book of the Bible, they encompass the vastness of God's character and the depths of human emotion and experience.

"They [the Psalms] are written to be prayed, recited, and sung—to be done, not merely to be read,"[xiii] according to Timothy and Kathy Keller in the introduction to the *Songs of Jesus: A Year of Daily Devotions in the Psalms.* Truly, the Psalms are a rich source for memorization and meditation.

Decide on Text Length

When I started memorizing, I decided to go with whole chapters. But don't let the idea of an entire chapter scare you off. I chose chapters because I wanted to avoid learning references. For instance, can you see advantages of recalling one reference, Psalm 27, for its fourteen verses rather than fourteen different book, chapter, and verse numbers for those fourteen verses?

If you decide not to start off with an entire chapter, that's fine. I encourage you to choose a passage of at least three or four verses. A passage gives some context, and it will provide enough food for thought for more than one day.

Choose the Passage

Like going to a buffet dinner, you want to put a little thought into the scripture passage you choose. After all, you may "chew" on it awhile.

Here's the good news: There's a huge selection of verses to choose from. The bad news? There's a huge selection of verses to choose from. If you have difficulty making decisions, see Appendix 1 for a list of passages that may work well for you. If you pick something and later get stuck, simply move on to another choice.

It's time to choose your first passage. Fortunately for you, you can't possibly make a mistake.

Choose When and How

Consider your lifestyle, your schedule. When is the best time to memorize? Usually I memorize while washing dishes or working in the kitchen, although posting a passage at my desk and in the bathroom helps reinforce it.

The decision of *how* you plan to memorize will influence the *when*. Will you look at the verse and repeat it multiple times? Do you have time to read it over and over (preferably aloud)? Would it work better for you to listen to the chapter multiple times, eventually learning it that way?

Your learning style should determine your decisions at this step. If you don't know your learning style, take a quick, online assessment. (See Appendix 2, point 3.4)

Meditate

Start meditating even if you only have one verse or one phrase memorized. Remember, you can meditate anytime, anywhere that your mind does not need to concentrate on tasks at hand. During a few minutes of my exercise time today, I thought about this phrase from I John 4:16 that I had recently memorized: *"God is love, and whoever abides in love abides in God, and God abides in him."*

As I went about my day, I took advantage of seconds and minutes of time that I could think about the verse. If I became unsure about wording, I could simply look at the printout of I John 4: 16-19 that I had placed in several locations of our home.

Tell Others

Tell others what God shows you about His Word, and explain how you are applying it. Regarding the person who delights in and meditates on God's Word, Psalm 1:3 says: *"He is like a tree planted by streams of water that yields its fruit in its season, and its leaf does not wither. In all that he does, he prospers."* The tree in this description refreshes and nourishes others. What you relate to someone else may encourage that person with a spark of hope or a morsel of truth. When you share with others, your vitality flourishes. Live as a benevolent tree to others.

Tell others about your new habit. Invite them to ask you about what God is doing in your life. You and others will grow spiritually.

Detailed Example of the Process

Let's take a few minutes to walk through the process, using what I did yesterday as an example. Some of what I did conforms to my goals, some doesn't. I admit, the process of memorization, review, and meditation challenges me on a daily—no, moment by moment—basis. Too often I choose the easy path and allow my mind to drift. But I strive for the goal of centering my thoughts on scripture as much as possible. (If you don't find this detailed explanation helpful, feel free to skip to the end of Chapter 3.)

Here's what I did yesterday. First, I studied. As I write this, I am memorizing 2 Corinthians 5, so I studied the next verse in the chapter, which was verse 4: *"For we that are in this tabernacle do groan, being burdened: not for that we would be unclothed, but clothed upon, that mortality might be swallowed up of life."* (KJV) I had started memorizing 2 Corinthians 5:4 the previous day. In addition, I had read the entire chapter in context and listened to it multiple times, so I found it familiar by this point.

After praying for the Spirit's guidance and instruction, I studied the verse using e-Sword Bible study software and recorded my findings in Study Notes. I listed the main words in the verse (a longer than usual list). Then I looked up each word in Strong's Dictionary and Thayer's Greek Definitions if I wanted more of an explanation. Here is what I came up with:

Tabernacle: a hut or temporary residence, that is, (figuratively) the human body (as the abode of the spirit)

Groan: to make (intransitively be) in straits, that is, (by implication)

29

to sigh, murmur, pray inaudibly: - with grief, groan, grudge, sigh.

Burdened: weigh down, depress

Unclothed: to cause to sink out of, that is, (specifically as of clothing) to divest; strip, take off from, unclothe

Clothed upon: to invest upon oneself, to put on over

Mortality: liable to death, mortal

Swallowed up: to drink down, that is, gulp entire (literally or figuratively); devour, drown

Life: of the absolute fullness of life, both essential and ethical, which belongs to God

Next I recorded a personal observation: *Considering that the physical body is just a temporary residence, if I elevate it to greater importance than it should have, that is similar to valuing material things (that will decay) over things that last.*

Then I read through the translations offered by e-Sword and chose two that fit well with the meaning of the words I had just researched:

"For truly, we who are in this tent do give out cries of weariness, for the weight of care which is on us; not because we are desiring to be free from the body, but so that we may have our new body, and death may be overcome by life." (BBE)

"While we live in this earthly tent, we groan with a feeling of oppression; it is not that we want to get rid of our earthly body, but that we want to have the heavenly one put on over us, so that what is mortal will be transformed by life." (GNB)

Following that, I read Albert Barnes' Notes on the Bible for verse 4 and copied part of it, underlining parts that especially spoke to me:

> Not for that we would be unclothed - Not that we are impatient, and unwilling to bear these burdens as long as God shall appoint. Not that we merely wish to lay aside this mortal body. <u>We do not desire to die and depart merely because we suffer much, and because the body here is subjected to great trials.</u> This is not the ground of our wish to depart. We are willing to bear trials. We are not impatient under afflictions. The

sentiment here is, that the mere fact that we may be afflicted much and long, should not be the principal reason why we should desire to depart. <u>We should be willing to bear all this as long as God shall choose to appoint. The anxiety of Paul to enter the eternal world was from a higher motive than a mere desire to get away from trouble.</u>

But clothed upon - To be invested with our spiritual body. We desire to be clothed with that body. <u>We desire to be in heaven, and to be clothed with immortality.</u> We wish to have a body that shall be pure, undecaying, ever glorious. It was not, therefore, a mere desire to be released from sufferings; it was an earnest wish to be admitted to the glories of the future world, and partake of the happiness which we would enjoy there.

That mortality might be swallowed up of life - On the meaning of the word rendered 'swallowed up.' The meaning here is, that <u>it might be completely absorbed; that it might cease to be</u>; that there might be no more mortality, but that he might pass to the immortal state - to the condition of eternal life in the heavens. The body here is mortal; the body there will be immortal; and Paul desired to pass away from the mortal state to one that shall be immortal, a world where there shall be no more death."[xiv]

Barnes' notes on I Corinthians 15:54 "Death is swallowed up in victory." (a similar phrase to the one in verse 4):

Is swallowed up - Κατεπόθη Katepothē (from katapinō, to drink down, to swallow down) means to absorb (Revelations 12:16); to overwhelm, to drown (Hebrews 11:29); and then to destroy or remove. The idea may be taken from a whirlpool, or maelstrom, that absorbs all that comes near it; and the sense is, that he will abolish or remove death; that is, cause it to cease from its ravages and triumphs.[xv]

Later, as I dressed and prepared for the day, I listened to John 15 and Psalms 62-63 several times until I could say the passages along with the audio. Although I try to daily review the chapters I have memorized in the past few months, due to some unusual circumstances, I had not kept up and my memory had grown rusty.

During the day I mulled over 2 Corinthians 5:1-4 and several other verses at random times. When I fixed our evening meal, I reviewed verse 4, my verse of study that morning. When I washed dishes later, I continued working on 2 Corinthians 5. Earlier, during our walk around the neighborhood, I explained to my husband that I was struggling with the passage. Since I memorize in King James Version, often I have difficulty with the wording. But if I persevere, I do eventually learn it.

As I showered and prepared for bed, I reviewed John 15. A beautiful mystery waiting to be unlocked and discovered, this passage has often occupied my conscious thoughts since I memorized it three months ago. In those moments of pondering, I saw a special application of this chapter.

Recently I had kept my stress level down with a realistic perspective of my to-do list. But last night the burden of my responsibilities hit me. I looked ahead to the rest of the week and saw I had scheduled far too many extra activities. Besides that, I needed to tackle several important tasks I should have done last week (or earlier).

I had just quoted most of John 15 about abiding in Christ, fruitfulness, abiding in Christ's love, and His joy in us. But in my anxiety over my schedule, I prayed, *God what am I doing wrong? Why do I have so much to do?*

It occurred to me that God desires fruitfulness, not busyness. So maybe He's most concerned that I live in His love, joy, peace, longsuffering, gentleness, goodness, faith, meekness, and temperance and express the same to others. Maybe whether I make a visit this week to a dear friend or wait until next month, or we remodel our kitchen this year or five years from now, or whether I attend a writer's group meeting in two days or not, is not the issue. In all I do, in all I am, if I am not living close to God's heart, my life is empty. What counts is what I am and Christ's life in me as I do whatever I do.

And with that insight I *should* have ended my day on a golden note, peacefully drifting off to sleep. Not so. My emotions would have none of it. Instead, after an hour of tossing in bed (with sporadic meditating), I got up. After an hour of bookkeeping on the computer, my emotions quieted, and I finally went to bed.

Yesterday was a typical day. Sometimes I made good decisions. Sometimes I didn't. But I try to keep God's Word in mind as much as possible, just sitting with it, allowing it to soak into the dark places, into the depths of my being.

Would you like to begin, but would like a little structure? See Appendix 4 for a 30-day Bible study on what the Word says about meditation while practicing the process of study, memorization, and meditation.

Please don't finish this chapter with a sigh and list of reasons why you can't meditate. Do obstacles obstruct your path? Let's see what we can do to clear them out of the way so you can experience blessings of a scripture-soaked mind. After all, up ahead, beautiful agates await.

4

Challenge Roadblocks, Detours, and Potholes

"What we love, we love to think of."[xvi]
Matthew Henry on Psalm 119:97

"Be careful how you think; your life is shaped by your thoughts."
Proverbs 4:23 GNB

MY EXPERIENCE WITH MEDITATION parallels my relationship with kale. A year ago I had never tasted the dark green leaf and didn't have any interest in adding it to my menu. Two colliding events changed everything.

First, I couldn't see well. In just months, my vision had noticeably deteriorated. Unusual recent physical changes in my eyes left the specialists confused.

Second, a medical professional advised me to "eat my greens." Greens supply large amounts of lutein, a nutrient essential for eye health. And kale boasts the greatest concentration. So, into our shopping cart it went. Then I had to decide how to prepare the kale. Cooked and seasoned or added to soup or a casserole? Or perhaps raw, in a salad, or disguised in a smoothie?

Despite the tough, curly texture and somewhat bitter flavor, I choose raw, in salad. Whether it's the main ingredient of salad or one of many veggies, I prefer this quick and easy method. Yes, its texture takes some getting used to. But with a little sea salt and garlic powder topped off with a drizzling of olive oil, I soon grew accustomed to kale. I hoped this new friend would make a difference in my vision.

A few months ago, we traveled to see yet another retina specialist, this one at the National Eye Institute in Bethesda, Maryland. It was still dark when we entered the spacious facilities. We clung to a speck of light, a hope that something could be found to arrest my declining vision and perhaps even restore what had been lost.

But after a taxing day of testing, we received jarring, suck-the-wind-out-of-you news. "I believe your retinopathy is genetic; if it is, there's nothing we can do. Even if it isn't genetic, but is autoimmune, we have no evidence that the medication we could give you would help," the specialist concluded.

After steadying myself, I asked the doctor about the many supplements I had made a habit of consuming, including kale. "It won't hurt and may help your overall health, but it won't benefit your vision."

And with that, the urgency of ingesting large quantities of kale evaporated. I still eat it. But now, it's by choice.

Thirty-five years ago, I started memorizing and meditating, not because I enjoyed it, but because I needed it (just like the kale). Other people had spoken into my life and convinced me that I needed a constant infusion and mega-doses of God's Word.

Not totally convinced of the outcome, I tried it anyway. I primarily reserved meditation for nighttime, while I found ways to memorize during the day. Little did I know that God would use meditation as the single greatest influence in my life for spiritual growth.

Meditation accomplished in my spirit and soul what detailing does to a vehicle. A car, maintained with just a superficial, occasional hosing down, may provide reliable transportation, but closer inspection will reveal dried insects, caked dirt, and interior stains. A detailing business will remedy all those areas. After a fresh coat of wax, the vehicle looks almost new.

God's Word, illuminating unkind words, selfish motives, wrong responses, and a slew of other sources of 'dirt' on soul and spirit, also cleanses, sanitizes, and purifies. Through His Word, God applies the shine to our lives of ministry to others, a godly example to our families, and a countenance expressive of trust and peace. As part of our spiritual maturing process, God seeks to remove us from the control of our emotions to the control of His Spirit, as guided by the Word.

Years ago, I met with someone who gave me some disheartening news. Once back home, I felt like retreating to my room for a good cry. I did go to my room, but one of the verses I had been memorizing and reviewing came to mind, *"My soul breaketh for the longing that it hath unto thy judgments at all times."* Psalm 119:20 (KJV).

My heart should be breaking with longing for God's Word, not for this, I realized.

Sure, I was still disappointed. But instead of allowing my emotions to rule the moment, I allowed God's truth to re-direct my hopes, changing me in the process.

Just last week, as He often does, God used His Word through meditation for my spiritual growth. Preparing to remodel our kitchen, a carpenter came to our home to give us ideas on our tight space. However, he didn't see any options unless we wanted to add on to the house.

His words immediately increased my expectations.

If we just had another $30,000, we could do it. That's really what we need, I fantasized.

A couple days later (and still thinking about an expanded kitchen), God used Psalm 62:11 to open my eyes to my need for contentment. *"Once God has spoken; twice have I heard this: that power belongs to God."* The verse didn't appear to speak to greed, but when I looked back at my study notes, I saw a relation. Barnes' notes on verse 11 referred back to the previous two verses:

> "The sentiment here is particularly important ... as the psalmist had shown, all other resources fail, and confidence is to be placed in nothing else for that which man so much needs; neither in people, ... not in oppressive acts - acts of mere power; not in plunder; not in wealth, however acquired ..."[xvii]

"And if I got a bigger kitchen, then what?" I asked my husband, when I told him about this the next day. "Will I be any happier?" I answered my own question: "No."

Through meditation of God's Word, I saw my wrong desires and again surrendered to His plan.

While meditation offers many opportunities for growth, obstacles may arise. If you have read this far, you obviously have a desire to meditate and probably have determined to do so. But once you are into the process, you may have questions. Or you may hit some rough waters. Let's look at some challenges that could hinder our resolve to meditate.

"I Just Can't Memorize" Roadblock

Do you remember your address? Do you recall your social security number? Of course you do! You can recite these tidbits of information because you place importance on them and repeat them often.

Biblical memorization is just remembering scripture. *How will I memorize?* you wonder, *I have such a poor memory.*

Perhaps memorization isn't your strong suit. Maybe learning massive passages would defeat you, but you *can* remember smaller bits. In my twenties, my young brain could memorize chapter after chapter. My mind now struggles to pack away just a few verses. But I can still memorize something.

Janet Pope, who has memorized over 150 chapters and even entire books of the Bible, first began memorizing at the age of thirty-five. With twenty-five years of experience in this discipline, she shared the following memorization tips with me:

1. Repeat, repeat, repeat. Repeat several times a day. If you still cannot remember, you simply need to repeat more often.
2. Start with a short passage (such as Psalm 1 or Psalm 100) and memorize one verse a day.
3. Find an accountability partner.

4. Review verses (previously memorized) while you do other things (while waiting, in the car, etc.)

5. Study the verse so you can intelligently apply it to your life. If time is limited, use a good study Bible such as John MacArthur's Study Bible.[xviii]

Most of the battle, as in anything else, occurs with our desires. We must focus our spiritual hunger on God's Word, not on quick fixes the world offers. When you get discouraged, remember your desire for God and His ways. Then determine again to engage in this profitable exercise.

"Life is Too Busy" Detour

We can't escape the hectic pace of life. But spiritual growth, unlike a microwave dinner, takes time. We need to drench our soul in God's Word. The good news? We can do this with as little as a five-minute-a-day investment plus some added intentionality. Consider this motto: *Take Five to Thrive*.

Why only five minutes? In a bare-bones approach, you could easily choose a verse or passage and print it out in five minutes. Sure, memorization and meditation come into play, but that can be done while you engage in your daily responsibilities. It could look something like this:

Take five minutes (or less) to pick out a verse for the day. If you don't have it memorized, print out several copies of the text. Place copies in areas where you will see them during the day. Whenever you see it, read the words. Try to repeat from memory as you go about your day. If you don't remember all the words, focus on one phrase at a time.

Think about the words as you prepare for the day. (If possible, say them aloud.) Consider them as you walk about your home or as you step out to your car or as you go into a store or work. Let them fill your mind when you prepare lunch and eat it. When you make phone calls, mull on them while you wait on hold. Meditate when you take a walk, sit outside, set the table for a meal, wash dishes, mow the yard, weed the garden, straighten up your living space, prepare for bed, and drift off to sleep.

Wherever you go, the words live with you. If you have only five seconds, let them zip through your mind. Sometimes you may be in a situation where you have five hundred seconds (for the curious, that's 1.38 hours). If so, let the words meander through your thoughts and heart, as you carefully examine every word, every facet, every treasure.

Consider this. If you have a busy lifestyle and want to maximize your moments, you will want to prepare yourself to meditate. Equipped, you can harvest the tidbits of your time.

Here's what I mean. Remember the last time you sat on the examination table waiting for the doctor while clutching the one-size-fits-none paper robe? Boredom ensues. Flip through a magazine? Out of reach. Ditto that for your phone. You have nothing to do but stare out at high windows that reveal leafless trees between mini-blinds. What a great time to meditate! Everything is quiet and you have the power to transform those minutes from *time wasted* to *time-invested in the eternal.*

When other things crowd in, remember that every minute invested in meditation turns to gold on God's balance scales. Meditation, like many of the other important priorities in your life, will not seem urgent, so we often easily dismiss it. But that doesn't mean it's not important. It just means we must intentionally add it to our lives.

Spiritual hunger and intentionality can maneuver around the roadblock of inability to memorize and the detour of lack of time. But how does one approach the pothole of lack of desire?

"I Don't Really Want To" Pothole

Visualize this: a room configured with identical chairs, a few worn magazines on end tables to rescue the desperately bored, and then add the desperately bored. Just sitting. Waiting. You know the score. You need to see a doctor or dentist for an appointment. Perhaps you have symptoms causing pain. Perhaps you came for a check-up.

Either way, you burn through thirty, sixty, or more minutes ...

waiting. Minutes you don't have to spare. Finally, your appointment ends and you can leave. But wait. They expect you to pay!

Why do you go? Not because you find the experience so attractive. If you went for a check-up, you didn't even go out of a felt need. You went for your future health and happiness.

At some point we all wander in a spiritual desert. We may simply need a good night's rest or a quiet walk. No matter how much "want to" we begin with, our desires will lag. When you find yourself with no desire to meditate or memorize, I would advise, "Meditate anyway." Some things we do simply because we should. Often the "want to" will follow the action. I realize, however, if we memorize and meditate regularly without any inner desire, spiritual and emotional exhaustion would eventually set in.

So, what's the answer? Literally, God is the answer. If we belong to Him and have His Spirit living in us, we *will* eventually experience benefits from meditation that will keep us coming back for more. God's Spirit will use His Word to speak to and commune with our spirit.

It comes down to a decision.

We decide what thoughts will fill our minds just as we choose what food to ingest. We find it easier to rip open a bag of chips and chow down than prepare a plate of carrot sticks. But soon afterward, the veggie eaters feel better and don't pack on extra pounds. Results motivate healthy eaters to continue with wise choices, just as comfort and assurance and wisdom from focusing on truth will entice biblical meditators to habitually feed on God's Word.

John Piper had this to say on lack of desire as he concluded his January 3, 1999, sermon (See Appendix 2, point 4.1):

> We struggle with Bible reading and memory and meditation because we don't find pleasure in it. We have other things we want to get to more. TV or breakfast or work or newspaper or computer. Our hearts incline to other things and do not incline to the Word. And so it is not a delight.[xix]

In his message the following Sunday, Piper explained how to resolve a lack of desire. The process he lays out to reach the goal of fruitfulness (from Psalm 1) contains the solution (See Appendix 2, point 4.2):

> "But the key to that kind of fruitfulness, we have seen in Psalm 1, is meditation on the Word of God day and night ... And the key to continual meditation is memorizing portions of the Scriptures so that we can keep them ever before us and savor them all the time. And the key to memorization and meditation is delighting in the Word of God ... [T]he key to delight is prayer. Or, more accurately, the key to delight is God's omnipotent, transforming grace laid hold on by prayer."[xx]

Do you see the progression? Fruitfulness results from meditation, which follows memorization, which springs from delight in or desire for God's Word, which comes through God's grace laid hold of in prayer.[xxi]

So, the key to meditation is prayer. Not rote petitions often recited as words that merely target the ceiling. But heart-desperate pleas that recognize a spiritual hunger and plead for God's transforming grace. When we get to this point and cry out to God in urgency, God will flood our hearts with grace and begin to grow in us a desire for Him and His Word.

The bottom line is: Do we yearn for God? If we do, we will want more of His Word in us. Just a quick read won't suffice. Meditation helps us internalize the Word so we can obey and grow. Like a thermostat, meditation regulates our spiritual growth. Meditation also functions as a thermometer—it measures our spiritual desire.

Perhaps you will encounter other roadblocks, detours, or potholes that threaten to deter you from meditating. Whatever hinders you, isn't it worth it to find a way to engage in this profitable pursuit? Often the turning point of a dilemma occurs when we stop making excuses for ourselves and simply determine to find a way to get it done.

Now that we have extracted the obstacles you may encounter, let's review how to begin this simple, life-changing adventure.

5

Finalize Preparations

"Meditation is attending deeply to God's truth,
purposes and revelation, so that the lies of the world are seen as lies,
and so the truth of God can pervade every aspect of our lives."[xxii]

Kyle Strobel

JOHN PIPER REFERS to meditation as having scripture on "the front burner" of his mind. I like that image, for it suggests the passage in Deuteronomy 6 when Moses exhorted the Israelites to follow God and to train their children in His ways. Specifically, verse 8 instructs, *"You shall bind them [God's instructions] as a sign on your hand, and they shall be as frontlets between your eyes."* In other words, keep these words ever before you, ready to access, on the front burner.

In one of his sermons, Piper shared an example of how keeping scripture on the front burner had impacted his life.

> Let me just give you an example of how this works in my own life. As I was coming to the end of the year and reading the final pages of the Old Testament in the Minor Prophets, I was moved by Micah 7:18. It is the foundation of a favorite hymn of mine, *Who Is a Pardoning God Like Thee?* by Samuel Davies. So I memorized it and carried it around on the front burner of my mind for several days. It says, *'Who is a God like*

thee, pardoning iniquity and passing over transgression
for the remnant of his inheritance? He does not retain
his anger forever because he delights in steadfast love.'

One of the insights that I discovered and tasted with
tremendous pleasure was that God does choose to be
angry, but his anger is limited. Why? Because he
'delights in steadfast love.' This means that anger is not
God's favorite emotion. He 'delights' in love. This has
huge implications – practical ones – about my life and
my own anger and love as I rest in him. And theological
ones, as I ponder the levels of willing in God: willing to
be angry in his holiness at sin, and yet not delighting to
be angry the way he delights to show steadfast love. I
was fed by this text for several days before I moved on
to another front-burner text.[xxiii]

A cursory reading of Micah 7:18 would not have yielded such a rich
feast. Nor would Piper have gained a greater understanding of God.
Think about it. How do we gain knowledge of God and His ways? How
can mere mortals cultivate intimacy with an invisible Creator? When we
keep His words—His revelation of Himself—on our minds, our
relationship with Him will deepen.

For instance, I have difficulty grasping the depths of God's love for
me. Read my journal account describing how meditation gave me a
renewed sense of His care:

This week I memorized and meditated on I John
4:16-20. While exercising, I thought about verse 16: *So*
we have come to know and to believe the love that God
has for us. God is love, and whoever abides in love
abides in God, and God abides in him. But my own
unhealthy thoughts kept intruding. Imaginations of
things I might do to impress others. Then the
incongruity occurred to me. *God* is love! What am I
thinking? Here I'm daydreaming about impressing
someone who might care about me a tiny bit when God

has poured all the love on me I need. But I would rather pick through a dumpster for a discarded, once-tasty morsel that just might appease my hunger instead of entering a banquet hall to feast on a hearty, delicious chicken enchilada dish with all the sides.

God's gentle, loving rebuke gave me a heightened awareness of His complete love for and acceptance of me. And when the unhealthy, self-defeating thoughts return? Then I remember, *"God is love,"* and I reach for that chicken enchilada.

Importance to Spiritual Growth: My 2016 Story

Recently I realized afresh how desperately I needed God's Word saturating my thoughts, day or night. I set a goal for 2016: gratitude. But how does one develop thankfulness? Believing I needed to focus on truth, I decided to review a collection of verses I had memorized years before on *The Truth that Sets Us Free* by Nancy DeMoss Wolgemuth.[xxiv] (See Appendix 2, point 5.1)

Even after re-memorizing these powerful truths, I would catch myself mulling over a mental list of recent (and not-so-recent) challenges in my life. My complaints centered on the time required to care for my elderly parents-in-law and their interests, the energy-sucking demands of our small business, my ever-present physical challenges with the limitations of rheumatoid arthritis and declining vision, the ocean that separates us from seeing our only grandchild, and the deep cavernous ache of losing a son at an early age. Negative thoughts dominated my inner conversation and extinguished any sprouts of gratefulness.

The tipping point came when I intentionally captured all the moments I could to review, remember, ponder, muse on, reflect on, and think about scripture. God's Word profoundly affected my spirit. I felt more thankful, even for the hard things that once formed my complaints. Gratitude began growing in my life for the opportunity to invest in family members who have invested so much in us, for the opportunity to add value to lives through our business, and for the lessons I am learning as I live with chronic health challenges. Besides that, I noticed a greater sensitivity to sin, neediness for God, compassion, trustfulness, and joyfulness. I loved God's Word more and temporal things less.

In addition, when I actively meditate on God's Word, my own thoughts evaporate. And that's good because my mind naturally gravitates to the untrue:

> "I'm no good."
> "God must not love me."
> "God has forgotten me."

I also tend to toward unhealthy thoughts and actions:

> complaining about circumstances,
> coveting what others have, and
> comparing myself to others.

Dwelling on scripture breaks my old, unhealthy introspections and sets me on a path of true, life-giving reflections.

Benefits Make Life More Meaningful

The agate treasure hunt Trent and I went on years ago added an extra dimension to our lakeside stroll, even though we sought a mere stone that would at best rate as semi-precious. If an agate hunt added interest to a walk on the beach, how much more could a quest for the knowledge and application of scripture add purpose and motivation to life?

Proverbs 2:1-5 encourages us to wholeheartedly seek God and His words: *My son, if you receive my words and treasure up my commandments with you, making your ear attentive to wisdom and inclining your heart to understanding; yes, if you call out for insight and raise your voice for understanding, if you seek it like silver and search for it as for hidden treasures, then you will understand the fear of the LORD and find the knowledge of God.*

God urges us to hold His words close and treasure them; He

counsels us to listen carefully to them not only with our ears, but also our hearts. Cry out with urgency and seek with intentionality. Then we are promised a greater understanding of Who God is and an awareness of His presence. Then we will attain that for which we were created.

Not only does living in scripture add meaning to my life and feed my soul, but it provides nourishment and refreshment for me to share with others. And that enriches my life.

Source of Wisdom and Encouragement for Others

With its 530 carats, the Cullinan 1 (or Star of Africa 1) ranked as the largest cut diamond in the world until dethroned in 1987. Each of the 74 facets of the pear-shaped Cullinan 1 flourishes its own radiance of beauty in its display case in the Tower of London.[xxv]

Likewise, scripture has a multi-faceted beauty with dozens or even hundreds of applications. As people share what they learn from the Word from the context of their unique personalities and circumstances, God's beauty blossoms in our eyes.

Often we long to encourage others—a dear friend in a tight place, a neighbor grieving a loss, or a family member adjusting to a health crisis. Where can we find words and thoughts that convey tangible hope? Only one place—God's Word.

After our son died, we connected with a suicide survivor support group in our area. (A *suicide survivor* is one of the family and friends of someone who has died by suicide.) By the following fall, other veteran members had left the group and recent suicide survivors took their place. In the meantime my husband had gathered some key players in our county to help organize a suicide prevention coalition. He had also created a presentation, "When Love is Not Enough," that we offered in our area.

Occasionally those in grief call us for help after a loved one ends his or her life. One of those calls came from a woman who identified herself as an atheist when I asked about church connection. I urged her to visit the support group. Beyond that, my mind blanked out. Pray with or for her? I didn't want to offend. Give her truth and hope from God's Word?

Perhaps that would annoy. Would sharing the Gospel sting her sorrowing heart? I simply didn't know.

I held off praying with her or sharing God's Word, hoping I would see her at the support group. If I could speak to her face-to-face, I could perhaps gauge her openness to spiritual things. Maybe she needed some time before the worst of the shock wore off and her heart could listen. After our loss, it took me, even as a Christian, at least two weeks before scripture penetrated the darkness and ministered to my needs.

In all, her call confirmed for me that God's Word holds the only meaningful hope for a hurting soul. For those willing to listen, scripture imparts a comfort not found elsewhere.

Recently, I witnessed God's Word comfort a hurting heart. I mailed a gift book of my writings to a recently-widowed friend. Meditation on scripture births most of my writings, including the ones in the book I sent her. Later, she sent me a beautiful thank you card with a handwritten note that said, in part, "The book is beautiful and the words echo the feelings in my mind and heart. When the heartache is so intense and the pain so great, I think I'm on a path that I can't make ... I know how desperate and needy I am ... So much of what you wrote is so true and applicable."

Review Actions to Take

Do you sense hunger pains? Remember, temporal things may satisfy a physical desire, but only the eternal can satisfy the deep desires of your soul. Now, just as a pilot does a quick run-down of his checklist before take-off, let's review the path to soul satisfaction one last time.

Decide to do it

I encourage you to act today. Believe in the power of decision. Don't get caught in the cesspool of excuses. Run to the spring of creative determination.

Andy Andrews' seven vital decisions form the bedrock of wisdom in his bestseller, *The Traveler's Gift: Seven Decisions that Determine Personal Success*. The third decision is "The Active Decision: I am a

Person of Action." He says in part:

> I can make a decision. I can make it now. A person who moves neither left nor right is destined for mediocrity. When faced with a decision, many people say they are waiting for God. But I understand, in most cases, God is waiting for me! He has given me a healthy mind to gather and sort information and the courage to come to a conclusion.[xxvi]

Despite your distractions, demands on your time, and even times of disinterest, determine to meditate. I've presented ideas to get started, so get in the cockpit and start your engines!

Pick the Passage

Have you started your list? If not, it's time to begin. Take a few minutes and choose a passage. Remember to consult Appendix 1 if you need ideas.

Study, Memorize, Meditate

Study the first verse in the passage. At a minimum, read the context—the handful of verses before and after your verse. Then maybe study a few key words. For a quick study, consult a study Bible.

Remember, memorization naturally results from repetition. Advancing age may require more repetition than it did in youth, but it's still possible. And it's worth every repetition it takes.

Once memorized, let that scripture fill your mind. Focus on it whenever possible. Tap into your wasted minutes and hours. Mine that time for eternal results.

Tell Others

Share blessings with others. Tell a friend about insights you have. Relate an application in a conversation with your spouse or children. Encourage another person to keep God's Word on the front burner.

Thank you for taking this Soul Pursuit journey with me. I pray that

God will use these words to encourage and instill a hunger within you for meditation. In closing, I'd like to share a prayer and a blessing for you.

Closing Blessing

As you fill your mind with God's Word, may ...
your awe of God,
your love for others,
your conviction over sin,
your sense of dependence and humility, and
your hunger for more of God ever
grow, develop, expand, intensify, spread, multiply, and surge forward,
making your life an ever-clearer reflection of Christ.
Amen

Thank you for reading my book. If you enjoyed it, won't you please take a moment to leave me a review at Amazon.com? Thanks!

Lynelle Watford

Appendices

Appendix 1: Suggested Passages to Memorize

Numbers 6:24-26: A blessing

Psalm 1: A comparison of a godly person to the wicked

Psalm 23: A psalm of comfort and assurance

Psalm 27: A psalm of focused intentionality on the Lord

Psalm 46: A psalm of trust, even in the most chaotic of times

Psalm 100: A psalm of joyous thanksgiving

Matthew 5:3-12: The Beatitudes

Romans 8:28-39: A declaration of God's love and sovereignty

I Corinthians 13: An exposition of the greatness of love

Galatians 5:16-25: The works of the flesh versus the fruit of the Spirit

Galatians 6:1-10: An exhortation to serve others

Philippians 3:7-14: The Christian's standing in Christ's righteousness

Colossians 1:12-20: Magnificent supremacy and headship of Christ

Colossians 3: Practical instruction for the Christian walk

Appendix 2: Online Resources: Memorization/Meditation

Chapter 2

Bible study resources:

> 2.1 Software--e-Sword free software: e-sword.net
>
> 2.2 Websites—
>> BibleHub.com-(probably closest to using e-Sword)
>> BibleStudyTools.com
>> Lumina.Bible.org

Chapter 3

Meditation Resources:

> 3.1 Institute in Basic Life Principles—
> The article, "How can I meditate on Scripture?":
> IBLP.org/questions/how-can-i-meditate-scripture
> Meditation worksheet:
> IBLP.org/questions/what-scripture-meditation-worksheet
> 3.2 Article "Biblical Meditation," J Hampton Keathley, III.
> Bible.org/article/biblical-meditation

Other Resources:

> 3.3 Janet Pope—
> Advice & encouragement on memorizing scripture,
> accountability groups: JanetPope.org
> 3.4 Free learning style assessment:
> How-to-Study.com/learning-style-assessment

Chapter 4

Sermons by John Piper:

> 4.1 "Meditate on the Word of the Lord Day and Night," January 3,
> 1999, includes John Piper's testimony on meditation:

DesiringGod.org/messages/meditate-on-the-word-of-the-lord-day-and-night

4.2 "Pray without Ceasing," January 10, 1999, explanation of the source of fruitfulness being the desire for God and how to get it: DesiringGod.org/messages/pray-without-ceasing

Chapter 5

Revive Our Hearts Resources:

5.1 "The Truth that Sets Us Free" Bookmark from *Lies Women Believe* by Nancy DeMoss Wolgemuth: ReviveOurHearts.com/articles/the-truth-that-sets-us-free

5.2 Buy the book, *Lies Women Believe and the Truth that Sets Them Free* by Nancy DeMoss Wolgemuth: ReviveOurHearts.com/store/product/lies-women-believe-and-the-truth-that-sets-them-free-special-offer

Other Resources:

Choosing verses for memorization and meditation:

Bible verses by topic and for every occasion. Includes reference and text of verses in various translations: Christianity.about.com/od/prayersverses/qt/bibleversesall.htm

Bible verses by topic with a feature to view in a multitude of translations and then navigate to other parts of the Bible: Biblestudytools.com/topical-verses

Meditation Resources:

Andrew Davis, senior pastor at First Baptist Church in Durham, North Carolina, encourages believers to practice 'extended memorization' or memorizing whole chapters or even entire books. Read about him at: TheGospelCoalition.org/article/skip-the-verse-memorize

Free download of book *Habits of Grace: Enjoying Jesus through the Spiritual Disciplines* (2016, David Mathis, Crossway, Wheaton, IL) with a good section on the interrelationship between memorization and meditation. See especially chapters 3 & 4: DesiringGod.org/books/habits-of-grace

PreceptAustin.org shares a vast conglomerate of information on God's Word including biblical meditation. See the collection of resources on meditation at: PreceptAustin.org/a_primer_on_meditation.htm

Appendix 3: Benefits of Meditation

Why should you meditate on scripture? Here are a few reasons from a logical point of view:

1. It keeps scriptures ever present in our mind, so we always have ready access to the Bible wherever we are.

2. It brings a constant supply of Truth unto our souls (our inner being so susceptible to the lies of self, Satan, and the world).

3. It allows us to fulfill God's original intent for our lives, to live in close relationship to Him, to abide in His Word.

4. During meditation, we think God's thoughts, not our own empty, untrue, or unhealthy thoughts.

5. It makes us more sensitive to our sin and our neediness for God.

6. It must bring pleasure to God's heart when we keep His Words uppermost in our minds.

7. It sharpens our minds so we can remember better in general.

I could go on, but you get the idea. Meditation would greatly benefit your spiritual life. Meditation would benefit *you*.

What does the Bible say about the benefits of meditation? Those who meditate will:

1. Prosper and be successful (accomplish mission and act wisely)— Joshua 1:8

2. Be like a fruitful tree that prospers (successful in mission or task)—Psalm 1:3

3. Have their soul cravings satisfied (similar to how rich foods satisfy our physical hunger)—Psalm 63:5-6

4. Praise God with joy—Psalm 63:5-6

5. Find delight and dependence on God's Word—Psalm 119:15-16

6. Receive comfort, stability, and wisdom in difficult situations—Psalm 119:23-24

7. Not focus on worthless ideas (worry, fear, revenge), but instead concentrate on the truth—Psalm 119:23-24

8. Love the Word—Psalm 119:47-48

9. Enjoy their relationship with God and God will also find enjoyment in the relationship—Psalm 104:34

10. Receive warnings of wrong ways and rewards of obedience—Psalm 19:11-14

11. Have wisdom and understanding, a desire to follow God's ways, and great joy in scriptures—Psalm 119:97-104

Appendix 4: 30-day Bible Study on Meditation

Meditation. It's a popular topic. But have you ever considered what God's Word says about it? Take the next thirty days to explore the Bible to discover what place the ancient spiritual discipline of meditation has in our contemporary, fast-paced lives.

Invite God into your thoughts—practice meditation. Experience God's blessings in your life and be a source of hope to others as you share your insights and blessings.

Each day, this study invites you to focus on one verse about meditation (reflection on scripture). Study the verse, memorize it (or at least one phrase for a longer verse), and meditate on it. Record your insights and how God used His Word to benefit you and others.

Ready? Grab your Bible study tools, and let's start![xxvii]

Get a printable version of the daily Bible study format and the list of scriptures for the 30-day Bible study at ForeverWaters.com.

DAILY FORMAT

FOCUS
(Verse to read, study, memorize, and meditate on)

Read the context

SEARCH AND STUDY

Look up the Hebrew or Greek meaning (use *Strong's Concordance*) for several of the main words:

#1

#2

#3

#4

Read the verse in other translations and/or look the verse up in a commentary. Record your observations.

Extra—rewrite the verse in your own words:

PURSUE

Print out several copies of the verse and place them in areas you will see them. Read the verse often and repeat, trying to memorize it.

As you have opportunity, meditate on the verse. Record your insights and blessings:

VERSES FOR 30-DAY STUDY

DAY 1

Verse: Joshua 1:8a, "This Book of the Law shall not depart from your mouth, but you shall meditate on it day and night, so that you may be careful to do according to all that is written in it...."

Context: Joshua 1:1-9

DAY 2

Verse: Joshua 1:8b, "For then you will make your way prosperous, and then you will have good success."

Context: Joshua 1:1-9

DAY 3
Verse: Psalm 19:14, "Let the words of my mouth and the meditation of my heart be acceptable in your sight, O LORD, my rock and my redeemer."

Context: Psalm 19:7-14

DAY 4
Verse: Psalm 119:48, "I will lift up my hands toward your commandments, which I love, and I will meditate on your statutes."

Context: Psalm 119:41-48

DAY 5
Verse: Psalm 5:1, "To the choirmaster: for the flutes. A Psalm of David. Give ear to my words, O LORD; consider my groaning." (Many translations render this as, 'consider my meditation'.)

Context: Psalm 5:1-8

DAY 6
Verse: Psalm 119:11, "I have stored up your word in my heart, that I might not sin against you."

Context: Psalm 119:9-11

DAY 7
Verse: Isaiah 26:3, "You keep him in perfect peace whose mind is stayed on you, because he trusts in you."

Context: Isaiah 26:3-9

DAY 8
Verse: Psalm 119:97, "Oh how I love your law! It is my meditation all the day."

Context: Psalm 119:97-104

DAY 9
Verse: Psalm 119:98, "Your commandment makes me wiser than my enemies, for it is ever with me."

Context: Psalm 119:97-104

DAY 10
Verse: Psalm 119:99, "I have more understanding than all my teachers, for your testimonies are my meditation."

Context: Psalm 119:97-104

DAY 11
Verse: Psalm 1:2, "but his delight is in the law of the LORD, and on his law he meditates day and night."

Context: Psalm 1:1-6

DAY 12
Verse: Deuteronomy 6:6, "And these words that I command you today shall be on your heart."

Context: Deuteronomy 6:1-9

DAY 13
Verse: Psalm 77:12, "I will ponder all your work, and meditate on your mighty deeds."

Context: Psalm 77:6-13

DAY 14
Verse: Psalm 145:5, "On the glorious splendor of your majesty, and on your wondrous works, I will meditate."

Context: Psalm 145:1-13

DAY 15
Verse: James 1:25, "But the one who looks into the perfect law, the law of liberty, and perseveres, being no hearer who forgets but a doer who acts, he will be blessed in his doing."

Context: James 1:23-25

DAY 16
Verse: Psalm 104:34, "May my meditation be pleasing to him, for I rejoice in the LORD."

Context: Psalm 104:31-34

DAY 17
Verse: Jeremiah 15:16, "Your words were found, and I ate them, and your words became to me a joy and the delight of my heart, for I am called by your name, O LORD, God of hosts."

Context: Jeremiah 15:16-21

DAY 18
Verse: Psalm 119:15, "I will meditate on your precepts and fix my eyes on your ways."

Context: Psalm 119:9-16

DAY 19
Verse: Psalm 119:16, "I will delight in your statutes; I will not forget your word."

Context: Psalm 119:9-16

·DAY 20
Verse: John 15:7, "If you abide in me, and my words abide in you, ask whatever you wish, and it will be done for you."

Context: John 15:1-8

DAY 21

Verse: Psalm 119:148, "My eyes are awake before the watches of the night, that I may meditate on your promise."

Context: Psalm 119:145-152

DAY 22

Verse: Deuteronomy 11:18, "You shall therefore lay up these words of mine in your heart and in your soul, and you shall bind them as a sign on your hand, and they shall be as frontlets between your eyes."

Context: Deuteronomy 11:13-21

DAY 23

Verse: Psalm 49:3, "My mouth shall speak wisdom; the meditation of my heart shall be understanding."

Context: Psalm 49:1-20

DAY 24

Verse: Psalm 119:78, "Let the insolent be put to shame, because they have wronged me with falsehood; as for me, I will meditate on your precepts."

Context: Psalm 119:73-80

DAY 25

Verse: Job 23:12, "I have not departed from the commandment of his lips; I have treasured the words of his mouth more than my portion of food."

Context: Job 23:10-12

DAY 26

Verse: Psalm 143:5, "I remember the days of old; I meditate on all that you have done; I ponder the work of your hands."

Context: Psalm 143:1-6

DAY 27
Verse: Psalm 119:23, "Even though princes sit plotting against me, your servant will meditate on your statutes."

Context: Psalm 119:17-24

DAY 28
Verse: Colossians 3:16, "Let the word of Christ dwell in you richly, teaching and admonishing one another in all wisdom, singing psalms and hymns and spiritual songs, with thankfulness in your hearts to God."

Context: Colossians 3:14-17

DAY 29
Verse: Psalm 63:5, "My soul will be satisfied as with fat and rich food, and my mouth will praise you with joyful lips,"

Context: Psalm 63:3-8

DAY 30
Verse: Psalm 63:6, "when I remember you upon my bed, and meditate on you in the watches of the night;"

Context: Psalm 63:3-8

[i] "You Need Hunger," Revive Our Hearts Radio, www.reviveourhearts.com/radio/revive-our-hearts/you-need-hunger-2/ (January 7, 2015)

[ii] Jonathan Berry, "The God Who Delights to Satisfy," http://satisfiedinchrist.com/the-god-who-delights-to-satisfy/ (March 13, 2016)

[iii] Charles H. Spurgeon, *The Treasury of David*, Psalm 1:2, e-Sword Software: Version 10.4.0 by Rick Meyers

[iv] Kyle Strobel, *Formed for the Glory of God: Learning from the Spiritual Practices of Jonathan Edwards*, (Downers Grove: InterVarsity Press, 2013), 118.

[v] http://www.dictionary.com/browse/meditation?s=t, accessed April 19, 2016.

[vi] Strobel, *Formed for the Glory of God: Learning from the Spiritual Practices of Jonathan Edwards*, 115.

[vii] Donald S. Whitney, *Spiritual Disciplines for the Christian Life*, (NavPress, 1997), p. 44

[viii] Doug McIntosh, *God Up Close: How to Meditate on His Word*, (Chicago: Moody Press, 1998), 45

[ix] "How can I meditate on Scripture?" accessed June 22, 2016, http://iblp.org/questions/how-can-i-meditate-scripture

[x] http://www.recoveringgrace.org/media/Bill-Gothards-Statement.png

[xi] J Hampton Keathley, III, "Biblical Meditation," accessed June 22, 2016, https://bible.org/article/biblical-meditation

[xii] Pope, telephone interview, May 2, 2016, 5 pm ET

[xiii] Timothy Keller & Kathy Keller, *The Songs of Jesus: A Year of Daily Devotions in the Psalms*, 2015, Viking, New York, viii

[xiv] Albert Barnes' Notes on the Bible, e-Sword software, on 2 Corinthians 5:4.

[xv] Albert Barnes' Notes on the Bible, e-Sword software, on 1 Corinthians 15:54.

[xvi] Matthew Henry, *Matthew Henry's Commentary on the Whole Bible*, accessed on 2014 version of e-Sword software & produced by Rick Meyers, Psalm 119:97

[xvii] Albert Barnes' Notes on the Bible, e-Sword software, on Psalm 62:11.

[xviii] Pope, telephone interview, May 2, 2016, 5 pm ET

[xix] Piper, Sermon from January 3, 1999, "Meditate on the Word of the Lord Day and Night," accessed June 22, 2016, http://www.desiringgod.org/messages/meditate-on-the-word-of-the-lord-day-and-night

[xx] Piper, Sermon from January 10, 1999, "Pray Without Ceasing," accessed June 22, 2016, http://www.desiringgod.org/messages/pray-without-ceasing

[xxi] Paul Tripp defines grace in his May 25, 2016 blog entry, "Hang in There," as 'everything we need to be what he [God] wants us to be and to do what he calls us to do in the situation where he has placed us,' from 2 Peter 1:3, "His divine power has granted to us all things that pertain to life and godliness .. ."

[xxii] Strobel, *Formed for the Glory of God: Learning from the Spiritual Practices of Jonathan Edwards*, 115.

[xxiii] Piper, "Meditate on the Word of the Lord Day and Night," accessed June 22, 2016.

[xxiv] (Get a downloadable list here. https://www.reviveourhearts.com/static/uploads/pdf/articles/TheTruthSetsFreeBookmark.pdf)

[xxv] Joseph Castro, "What is the World's Biggest Diamond?", Live Science, April 29, 2013, accessed June 23, 2016, http://www.livescience.com/29147-worlds-biggest-diamond-largest-diamonds.html

[xxvi] Andy Andrews, The Seven Decisions that Determine Person Success," PDF accessed July 28, 2016 at https://www.andyandrews.com/downloads/print/AA_SevenDecisions.pdf

[xxvii] Bible study helps, either online or software (such as e-Sword) or study Bible, or individual books (Bible, concordance, commentaries, etc.). See point 2.2 under Appendix 2. All three suggested sites provide Strong's Concordance, several translations, and commentaries.

About the Author

Lynelle (Lyn) Watford lives in St. Joseph, Michigan, a quaint town on Lake Michigan. Besides writing, Lyn does bookkeeping and assists with Tech Help, the Watford's computer training and service business. Trent and Lyn are also involved with suicide prevention. Their older son is married and has a daughter; he serves the United States in the Air Force as a C-130J pilot.

Discover Other Titles by Lynelle Watford

Waters of Refreshment:
A Collection of Poetry and Photography

This 5 x 7 inch softcover book is perfect for a small gift to someone who needs a dose of encouragement. Eighteen pages of brilliant color and the author's favorite poems, all based on portions from God's Word are included in this collection. (Compiled November 2011)

Out of the Ashes: Hope
Thoughts of Hope for Hurting Hearts

The stunning beauty of Yellowstone and Glacier National Park adorn the pages of this 8 x 8 inch hardcover book. Just as the photography is a feast for the eyes, so the poetry and scriptures are nourishment for the soul. This 20-page collection of writing includes specially selected nuggets from the journal entries written in the first nine months after Lynelle's son died. If your heart is hurting, you will be validated and reassured as you peruse these pages full of transparency, honesty, and hope. (Compiled November 2011)

Out of the Desert: Refreshment
A collection of refreshing poems and reflections
birthed in the desert of pain

The photography in this 8 x 8 inch hardcover book relates to water--lakes, rivers, streams, and waterfalls--for all give a visual representation of refreshment. Likewise, the poetry and prose focus on refreshment of the spirit. In a pain-filled year of emotional, physical, mental, and even spiritual distress, God was there and gave insights into His Word. Whether your personal desert is pain, loneliness, financial need, or something else, your heart will connect with the pain expressed and will exult in the refreshment offered in these writings. (Compiled in the fall of 2012)

Out of the Storm: Peace
A journey to peace illustrated with poetry, prose, and photos

Highlighting selections from Lynelle's 2013 journal, the author shares her desire for peace after a deep loss. Journey with the author from the point of seeking to an unexpected realization about peace. The scripture and writing focusing on peace in this 8 x 8 inch hardcover book give insights to those who are seeking resolution with the inevitable difficulties in life. (Compiled in September 2014)

Connect with Me

ForeverWaters.com

ForeverWaters.com/blog

Please email if you would like to receive Lynelle's blog and updates:
Lyn@ForeverWaters.com

61073429R00044

Made in the USA
Lexington, KY
27 February 2017